BIG CITY PORT

by Betsy Maestro and Ellen DelVecchio

illustrated by Giulio Maestro

Four Winds Press
Macmillan Publishing Company · New York
Collier Macmillan Publishers · London

Macmillan Publishing Company
866 Third Avenue, New York, N.Y. 10022
Collier Macmillan Canada, Inc.
Printed in the United States of America
10 9 8 7 6 5 4 3 2
Library of Congress Cataloging in Publication Data
Maestro, Betsy.
  Big city port.
  Summary: Text and illustrations describe the unceasing
activity at a busy seaport, including the coming and
going of various ships and the moving of cargo by big
machines.
  1. Harbors—Juvenile literature. [1. Harbors]
I. DelVecchio, Ellen. II. Maestro, Giulio, ill.
III. Title.
TC205.M27 1985   387.1   85-4339
ISBN 0-02-762110-3

FOR ALI, DANIELA, AND MARCO

A big city port is a busy place.
Boats and ships come into the port
to load and unload.
It is a safe place for them to dock.

Freighters, tankers, and passenger liners
are large ships that come into the port.

The smaller tugboats, ferryboats, and fishing boats come, too.

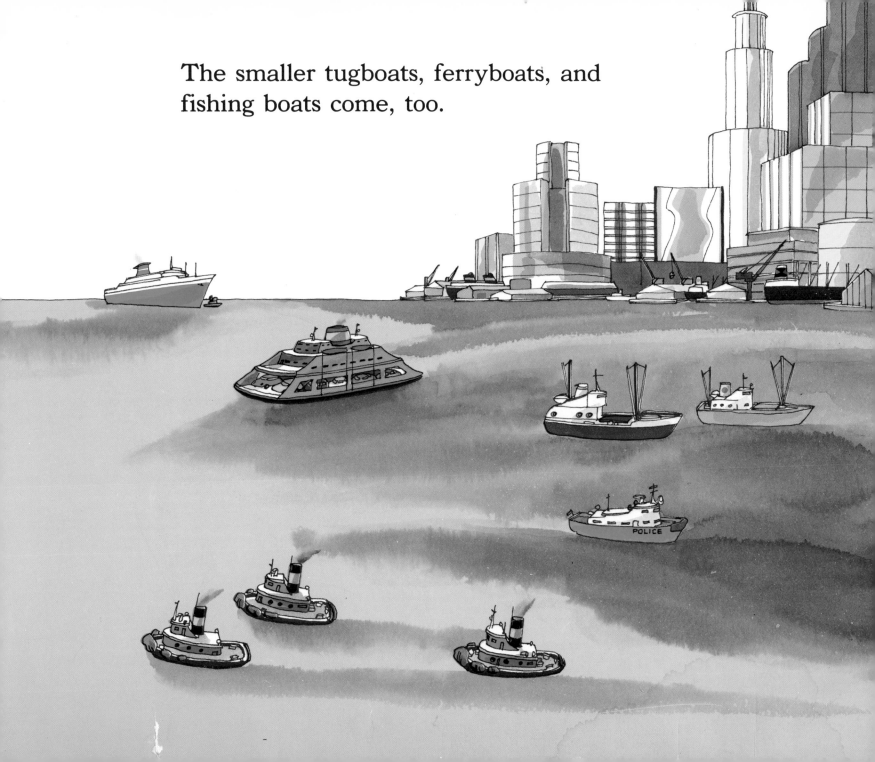

Large ships carry heavy loads.
A freighter is bringing coffee to the city.
The tanker is coming into port loaded with oil.
The ocean liner is arriving full of passengers.

Tugboats push and pull each big ship
through the harbor to the docks.
Big ships cannot turn and move in the small places
near the piers without help.

At the dock the freighter is unloaded.
Workers use big cranes to lift the sacks
of coffee beans out of the hold and
onto the pier.

Other freighters are unloaded at nearby docks.
Many different machines are used to move
their cargoes onto the docks.
Boxes, barrels, and bales are everywhere.

Everyone is busy on the docks,
working to move the cargo.
Some of it is loaded onto trucks and trains.
The rest is moved into large
storage sheds on the pier.

The big oil tanker has docked nearby, and the oil is pumped underground into big tanks on the dock.

Gasoline and fruit juice are unloaded
from other tankers.

The ocean liner has docked, and the passengers
are getting off.
Workers are unloading luggage.
Cars and taxis will take the people into the city.

Many smaller boats come into port.
Ferryboats go back and forth across the harbor.

They carry people and cars from one side
to the other.

Fishing boats go out early in the morning.
They will return full of fish at the end of the day.
The fish will be sold in markets in the city.

Many people control the traffic in a busy port.
The Captain of the Port is in charge
of all the boats and ships.

The captain on each boat or ship must follow directions and obey safety rules and signals.

There are other people who help to keep
the port safe.
Harbor police patrol the water and the piers.
Fire fighters help to put out fires and
clean up oil spills.
The fireboats are like floating fire engines.

The port never closes.
Workers are busy all day and all night.

At night very bright lights help them to see
so they can do their jobs.

A big city port is an important place.